ISBN 978-0-9905599-0-0

This book is Available at major on line book retailers
And through the publisher

Nancyorlando-books.com
Cincinnati, Ohio

Check our site for bookstore terms

Where's Pumpkin?

By Nancy Orlando

Illustrated by Debbi Kern

Contents

Preface and Dedication

I found Pumpkin on the Internet. I know
she was picked up by the SPCA in Cincinnati,
Ohio and discovered by a volunteer with a Shih
Tzu rescue group. The rescue group placed her
in a foster home until she could be adopted. She
is a wonderful little dog but is so frightened by so
many things. It is hard to watch her when she
hears a storm or loud noise. I shudder to think
about how she became so terrified. "WHERE'S
PUMPKIN?" is my idea of what may have

happened before I adopted her. Pumpkin tells her story in this format due to the many requests from our young reader fans for a chapter book.

There is a lesson to be learned from "WHERE'S PUMPKIN?" First, there is the obvious. Wonderful, loving pets can be found among the thousands of stray, homeless animals waiting in shelters and foster homes for a forever family to love and be loved by. Always check the local SPCA and rescue groups when looking for a new pet. Your new best friend is eagerly waiting for you to take him or her home so the shelter or foster home can make room for another needy animal.

Second, every pet should ALWAYS wear a collar with a tag bearing all the information necessary to return the pet to its owner, in addition to a microchip. Collars and tags come off at bath time, but there would be no story if Missy, (or whatever her name was) had a microchip or her collar and tags had been replaced as soon as the bath was over.

"WHERE'S PUMPKIN?" is dedicated to the devoted people at the Cincinnati Society for the Prevention of Cruelty to Animals and related groups in other communities and to the extraordinary efforts of the volunteers with the Breed Rescue Groups. Thanks to the commitment of all these wonderful people who rescue animals needing care, I was able to adopt

this precious fur baby and make her a part of my

family and my life.

I hope you enjoy "WHERE'S PUMPKIN?"

Part of your purchase price will be given to the

Cincinnati SPCA to help them protect more

animals in need. Thank You!

Chapter 1

I Just Ran

Hi there! My name is Pumpkin. I used to be called Missy. I was happy living with a really nice lady. Then I did a dumb thing. Did you ever make a mistake and do something really dumb? You can be very sorry you did it, but that doesn't help. You can't take back a mistake.

One sunny afternoon I really goofed. I had just had my bath and was sitting on my back steps to dry off. Nice Lady was combing and brushing my hair. She said she was sorry she had put off my grooming for such a long time. My hair was too long. I really needed a haircut. That didn't worry me. The lady who groomed me was very nice and always gave me a treat when she finished.

I watched Nice Lady watering the pots of flowers lined up on the patio. I had lived with her for over a year. She picked me out of my litter over my two sisters and one brother. I was the only champagne colored one. She thought I was pretty and smart, so she took me home with her.

We had a big back yard with a chain link fence all the way around it. I could play there any time I wanted to. I just barked to go out or to come in. Life was really good. I could stand at the gate and see people passing the front of the house. Sometimes I barked at them, but mostly I just watched and wondered where they were going. I thought it must be exciting to be on the other side of that gate.

That day, Nice Lady opened the gate so she could carry a pot of flowers to the front yard. "Stay," she said and pointed at me. She set the pot of flowers on the sidewalk so she could close the gate. I was so excited that the gate was open, I just took off running. I don't know why I ran. I just ran.

I could hear Nice Lady calling me, but I was so excited, I kept running. I ran past the neighbor's house and stopped for a moment to look back. Nice Lady was running after me. I thought this was a new game, so I ran faster. I ran across the street and saw a squirrel between two houses. I chased the squirrel, but it ran faster than I could. I ran until I was so tired I had to stop to rest.

I was panting, and I wanted a drink of water. I turned and looked for Nice Lady. I thought I would jump into her arms and go home for a cool drink of water, but she was nowhere in sight. I tried to figure out where I was. The houses on this street didn't look like the houses I could see from my fenced back yard. They were bigger, and the yards were bigger.

I really wanted to go home, but I didn't know where I was. I was so confused. Did I cross that street? Did I run through that yard?

Nothing looked familiar to me. Did Nice Lady wonder where I was? Oh, how I wanted to go home.

Chapter 2

I'm Tired and Thirsty

I walked behind one of the big houses. It had a beautiful back yard filled with flowers and bushes. There was a bench by a pond of water. Water! I was so happy to see water. I leaned over and lapped up some water. It was warm from the sun and didn't taste as good as the cool fresh water Nice Lady gave me, but it was water. I got a big drink and looked for a place to lie down and rest.

There was a bench under a tree near the pond. It was shady and cool there, so I decided I would rest for a little while and then find my way back to Nice Lady. I think I fell asleep the minute I put my head down.

When I woke up, the sun was setting. I stretched and almost forgot where I was. I thought about my red bowl filled with food in Nice Lady's kitchen. I was hungry, but there was nothing there to eat so I drank more water. At least I wasn't thirsty.

I started to walk away when I saw a man walking on the other side of the street. I thought maybe he could help me find Nice Lady. When I ran up to him, he stomped his foot and yelled,

"Scat." Then he kicked me. I moved just in time.

He didn't kick me very hard. I just wanted to go home, and I didn't know why the man would kick me. I was really scared.

It was getting dark, and the air was getting cooler. I thought about the warm soft spot at the foot of Nice Lady's bed. I wondered where I would sleep this night. Maybe I could go back to the bench beside the pond, but I had walked so far and didn't know how to go back there either.

Then I felt it. Rain! I thought about the shower in Nice Lady's bathroom. Sometimes, when I got in the mud at the edge of the garden, she put me in the shower to clean off the mud, but that water was warm. Rain water is cold.

I ran behind the nearest house. There was a wooden deck by the back door. I darted under it. The rain was coming in between the boards, but at the back of the deck near the house, it was dry. I huddled in that narrow space. I curled up and tried to stay dry. I was there for a very long time. I was cold and I was hungry, and I was afraid I would never find Nice Lady again.

The rain didn't stop. I huddled close to the house all night. Finally, it was morning. There was a dim light in the sky. I could not see the sun because of the clouds and the rain, but everything was a little lighter. It was still raining. Even the area close to the house was getting wet. In the distance there was the rumble of thunder.

Chapter 3

The Storm

I remembered hearing thunder before. It was a sound I really didn't like. I used to hide under the big bed until it stopped, but there was no place to hide out here. Then I saw a big flash of lightning. I was so scared my whole body began to shake. I had to find a safe place away from the noise and light flashes. I ran from the deck and back to the front yard. I ran through several yards and stopped under a bush for just a minute to catch my breath. Then I heard the thunder again. It was even closer, and the rain was coming down harder. I ran as hard as I could to find a place to hide.

I ran for what seemed like a long, long time. My hair was soaked and clinging to me. The rain was so cold, I couldn't stop shaking. Then I spotted an open garage door on one of the houses. I was frantic. I ran into the open space and huddled in the corner at the back of the garage. I was so wet the water puddled around me on the floor.

At least I was out of the rain. I found a pile of rags that were probably used to wash the car. I pawed at them and pushed them into a pile I could curl up on.

I don't know how long I lay there. I listened

to the storm and shook and shook.

Finally, the thunder and lightning stopped,

and the rain was not as heavy as before. I went

to the front of the garage and looked up and

down the street. There was no place in sight that

looked safe, so I went back to the pile of rags and lay down.

After a while, I could hear people talking in the house. I could smell delicious smells coming from the kitchen just behind the door at the back of the garage. I sniffed and sniffed. I was so hungry, and that odor from the kitchen smelled so good. I went to the garage door and stepped out onto the driveway. The rain was still coming down hard. It made a river of water run across the driveway. I ran out to get a drink and drank all I could hold. I shook off as much rain as I could and went back to the pile of rags. I was so tired I fell asleep right away.

I woke up when I heard the door from the kitchen open. A young boy came out pulling on a raincoat. He called over his shoulder, "Mom, Denny brought my English book home in his book bag to keep it dry. I'm going to get it so I can do my homework. Be right back."

"Come straight home," a woman's voice called from the kitchen. The boy looked friendly. I thought about running up to him. Maybe he would pet me and make me feel better, and maybe he would give me something to eat. Then I thought about that man on the street. What if the boy was mean too? I stayed very still and quiet until he ran from the garage.

In a few minutes, he came back and ran into the house. Suddenly there was a loud strange sound and the big garage door began to close. All I could do was stare and shake all over. Everything that had happened that day was so scary. I just couldn't move. The door slammed down, and all was dark and quiet. I sat there for a very long time. The house became very quiet, so I lay down and tried not to think about how hungry I was. I finally fell asleep but woke with the sound of the big garage door opening. A man came out of the house and got into the car. I was terrified when I heard the engine start.

Chapter 4

Running Again

I ran out of the garage and through the grassy yards as fast as I could go. I passed a lot of houses, but I was too afraid to stop. I came to a street and ran to cross it. Then I heard the car. It was very, very close, and the tires were squealing as the driver slammed on the brakes trying not to hit me. I dashed for the other side of the street. The car was so close I could feel the air rush past me like a strong wind. I ran to a bush and sat there. I was shaking and so scared.

I just wanted to be with Nice Lady and be safe in my fenced in back yard. How could I find my way home?

The sun was up and the sky was clear. I walked slowly along the front of the houses, hiding under bushes when a big yellow school bus stopped to pick up children who came out of the houses along the way. I started looking at the back yards, hoping I could find another pond with some water. I walked behind a big brick house.

Suddenly, a great big black dog came after me.

He was hooked to a big chain and could not come very far.

I backed away from him. I could hear him growling, and I saw his big teeth snapping at me.

I turned and ran as far and as fast as I could. I sat under a bush to calm down. I looked behind another house.

A woman wearing a bathrobe was putting seed into a bird feeder. She didn't notice me watching her. She went into the house and came right back out with a piece of bread. She tore it into small pieces, tossing them into the yard for the birds and went back into the house. I ran to one of the pieces of bread and gobbled it up. Then I ate the other pieces too. It was just bread, and there wasn't much of it, but after such a long time with nothing to eat, it really tasted good. There were no fences around the back yards in this area so I walked along the back of the houses looking for something to eat and some water. I stopped to rest and listened. There was noise coming from a back yard just up the street. It sounded like water.

I ran toward the sound. Then I saw it – a beautiful water fountain spraying water into a pond. I ran to the edge of the pond. I was about to get a drink when I saw my reflection in the water. I remembered how Nice Lady would brush me after my bath and put me in front of a mirror in the hall to show me how pretty I was. The reflection in the pond didn't look a bit like the one in Nice Lady's mirror. I wasn't pretty at all. My hair was dirty and matted. Even Nice

Lady would not call me pretty now. I got a drink from the pond and walked up the street.

I walked and walked. It was a nice day but I was so tired and my feet were really sore. Would I ever find Nice Lady and my fenced in back yard? I thought about the soft warm big bed. Where would I sleep tonight? All the garage doors I passed were closed. I rested under a bush when I was too tired to walk. I had to keep trying to go home so I kept walking.

Finally, the sun was going down. I had to find a place to spend the night. I was cold and so hungry. I went behind some bushes in the front of one of the houses. There were a lot of dried leaves between the bushes and the house. At least they made a soft place for me. The bricks on the house were still warm from the sun so the night air didn't feel quite so cold. I didn't sleep much. I couldn't forget how hungry I was or how frightening everything was. In the morning I started out again.

Chapter 5

I Hear Children

I walked and walked for a very long time. I had to cross several streets but I was very careful. I made sure there were no cars in sight before I quickly ran to the other side. I was very tired. Even the pads on my feet hurt. I needed a place to rest. I could see a very tall chain link fence around the corner, and I could hear happy voices of children coming from somewhere beyond the fence. I remembered the children in the house next to Nice Lady. Sometimes they would come into the back yard and play ball with me. I ran toward the happy voices. Maybe they would be nice like the children next door.

There was a big opening in the fence that led to a playground and a school. I ran straight to a boy sitting by himself under a tree next to the teeter-totters. "Hi doggie," he said. He held out his hand for me to smell and said, "I won't hurt you."

I sniffed the boy's hand. "Are you lost?" he asked. He said I looked like I needed someone to take care of me. He put his sandwich down and patted me on the head. I sniffed at his sandwich. I could smell peanut butter. It smelled so good and I was so hungry. "Would you like a bite?" he asked. He tore a piece of the sandwich off and

held it out to me. I tried to be polite, but I was so

hungry I grabbed it. I didn't chew.

I just gulped it down. "Whoa," said the boy. "You shouldn't eat so fast!"

A little girl came from the teeter-totter and said, "Who's your friend?" "I don't know her name," the boy answered. "I think she must be lost. She seems to be a pretty nice dog, and she's really hungry too."

"Here, you can have my cookie." The girl put a small cookie on the ground in front of me. I ate that cookie so fast. A loud bell rang, and most of the children ran toward the building. "We have to go inside now. If you stay here I will take you home with me after school," said the boy.

Chapter 6

Something to Eat!

I knew the word "Stay," but I wasn't sure what he wanted me to do. I sat under the tree and watched the boy run to his teacher at the door of the school. All the children gathered around her. Someone must have told her about me because they pointed at me and started to walk toward me. I knew the children were nice, so I ran to meet them. I ran to the boy who gave me a bite of his sandwich. I was so happy, for the first time since I ran through the gate. My tail was wagging so hard I felt like my whole body was wagging. The boy put his hand on my head.

The teacher held her hand out for me to sniff. Then she put her hand under my chin and lifted my head so she could see my face. "This dog was someone's pet," she said. "I don't know why she is running loose, but I'll bet someone would like to have her back. We will give her some food and water and call the SPCA to pick her up. They will find her owner or find her a new home. Tommy, you go to our room and get that pretty bowl off the window sill. Fill it with water and bring it here. Billy, the dog seems to like you, so you stay here while I go to the cafeteria and find something for her to eat."

In a few minutes, the teacher returned with a paper plate with pieces of a grilled cheese sandwich and a cut up hot dog. She put the plate down in front of me. Tommy came with the bowl of water and set it down next to the plate of food.

"You children stay with her," said the teacher. "I'm going in to call the SPCA and see if they can pick her up right away."

I was so excited. I lapped the water. It was cool, like the water Nice Lady gave me. I drank until I was satisfied. Then I tasted a piece of hot dog. It was so good I ate all the hot dog pieces as fast as I could. Then I turned my attention to the grilled cheese sandwich. My tummy felt much better, so I ate a little bit slower. I put my foot on the plate to hold it still while I licked every inch of that plate as clean as new.

The teacher returned and said the man from the SPCA would be there in about an hour. "I don't want her to run off." she said. "I have permission from the principal to hold our reading class outside today. That way we can keep the dog here until he arrives. I want you to go to our room and get your reading books." The children started to run to the building. "Quietly," called the teacher.

The children carried their books to the big tree. They sat in the shade. The teacher brought the water bowl and sat it under the tree for me. "There," she said. "I think this will be fun."

Billy held up his hand and asked, "What is the SPCA?"

The teacher replied, "That is the Society for the Prevention of Cruelty to Animals. They

rescue animals from people who abuse them, and

they help animals that are lost and have no one

to take care of them, like this little dog."

"Who would like to read first?" the teacher asked. A girl with a striped shirt held up her hand. "Thank you, Betsy," said the teacher. "Read the first two pages, please."

Chapter 7

Help Is Coming

I sat beside the teacher and listened to the children read. They had nearly finished the story when a man walked toward us carrying a net on a long stick. He asked, "Is this the dog I'm supposed to pick up?"

"Yes," replied the teacher, "but you won't need that net. She is a very pleasant little lady and very well behaved."

"That's good to know," replied the man. "Many times strays are sick or afraid and are very hard to catch." He picked me up with one

hand and held me close to his chest.

"Goodbye, little doggie," called one of the children.

"Goodbye, little doggie," the others called out.

The man said, "She will get a bath and a good grooming. Our vet will check her to be sure she is healthy. If her owner doesn't come in, I am sure she will have a new home in no time. Thank you for calling us."

He carried me to his truck. It was parked on the street in front of the tall fence. There were cages at the back of the truck. Several of them had dogs in them that were barking loudly. One of them was big like the dog that had run me out of his yard. I hoped this man wouldn't let the dog hurt me. I tried to snuggle closer to the man, but he put me in one of the cages. I was so scared I started shaking again.

"It won't be long until we are back at the shelter," the man said as he locked the door on my cage.

The dogs stopped barking when the truck began to move. When we reached the Shelter, the man backed the truck up to the back of the building. I was still shaking when he opened my cage and carried me inside.

"I have a special one for you today" he said to the woman in the office. "When she has a bath and a good grooming, this one will be a real beauty. You take her, and I'll put the others in kennels," he said and went to get the other dogs.

When he returned, the woman already had me in a sink full of warm, bubbly water. She worked the shampoo into my fur and rubbed my skin with her fingers.

It felt so good I closed my eyes and just relaxed. The lady asked, "Feels good, doesn't it?" I wished I could talk so I could tell her how much I was enjoying that bath.

After the bath, the lady dried my hair with a blow dryer. "You really need a haircut," she said. "You are shaggy and matted." She brushed out the tangles while she dried me and used the clippers to trim my hair. "You are a beautiful little lady," she said when she had finished. "Let's get you something to eat and drink while we wait for the vet to check you out." She put me in a big fenced in pen and closed the door.

I checked out the space. There were two bowls at the side of the pen. They were already filled with food and water. I took a bite of the

food. It was good, but I was nosier than I was

hungry. The food at the school had filled me up.

I walked to the back of the pen. There was a

small door there. I wasn't sure I should go

through it. This seemed like a safe place to be

while I waited for Nice Lady to find me. Would I

be able to get back in if I went through that door?

I poked my head through the door and

looked about. There was another pen with a

fence around it on the other side, but it was

outdoors. I went outside and quickly squatted to

pee and ran back inside. There was a big soft mat

in the pen. I sat for a moment, and then I

stretched out on it. I was so tired I fell asleep immediately.

I woke up when I heard a soft voice talking to me. "Did you have a nice nap?" a woman in a white uniform asked. She patted me on the head. "Would you like to visit my office?" she asked. She gently picked me up and carried me down the hall to her office and stood me on a metal table. She seemed nice but the table was cold, and the light in the room was so bright it hurt my eyes. There were strange smells I didn't understand too. Everything was so frightening.

She picked up a clip board and a pen. "What name shall I put on your medial record? Let me see. Your color is really different. The tips of your fur are almost orange. Let's just call you Pumpkin for now." She wrote something on a paper on the clipboard. The woman ran her hands over my body. She looked into my ears, checked my eyes, and listened to my heart and lungs. Then she carried me to a scale in the next room and weighed me. "Just a little light," she said. "Two or three days with food and water, and that weight will come back. I think you haven't been lost too long. You are very healthy for a stray. You are a lucky little lady. Maybe your owner will come in looking for you." She made notes on the medical record and took me back to my pen.

Chapter 8

I'm Rescued

The pen in the shelter was really comfortable. Everyone was very nice to me, and I had plenty to eat and drink. I could sleep on my mat any time I wanted, and I could go to the outdoor part of my pen anytime I needed to. Several days passed. This was not a bad place to be, but I still wanted to find Nice Lady. I wanted her to hold me on her lap and tell me she loved me. I missed her so much. I looked for her every day when people came through.

Every afternoon, people visited the shelter. They walked down the hall in front of the pens and looked at all the dogs. Sometimes they would ask to see one of the animals closer. They would go to a visitor's room, and the dog would be taken to them for a visit. Sometimes they would adopt the dog and take it home with them. I could not be adopted for a few days to give my owner a chance to claim me. It would be so nice to go home. I wondered how far away Nice Lady was and hoped she would look for me at this shelter, but Nice Lady didn't come.

The first day I was put up for adoption, a lady came through who volunteered with a Shih Tzu rescue group. She asked to see me. She really checked me out. She looked at my head and checked the shape of my body. She looked at my obvious under bite, the way my lower teeth show. "I think you are a Shih Tzu lady who needs to be rescued," she said to me.

I was returned to my pen while the lady went to the front desk to make the arrangements for the rescue group to take me and find a home for me.

It wasn't long before the lady came back to my pen. She put a collar and a leash on me and led me down the long hall to the front door. She put me in a travel cage on the back seat of her car. "Now I have to find a foster home for you until a forever home is available. You are so cute

I'm sure you will have a new home very soon. For now, you can visit my house."

It wasn't very long before the car turned into a driveway and pulled into a garage. I could hear the big garage door close. It was frightening. Was I going to be closed up in a garage again? The lady lifted me out of the carrier and put me down on the garage floor. "You're shaking," she said. "No need to be scared. No one is here but Sally and me, and neither one of us bites. Come on in." She held the door to the house open. "Sally wants to meet you."

I discovered Sally was a dog who looked enough like me to be my sister. She was just about the same size and very happy to have company. She sniffed at me. Then she crouched down on her front feet with her rump in the air ready to pounce. I wasn't sure just how to deal with Sally. I hadn't played since I ran from Nice Lady, but Sally was determined.

"Sally," the woman scolded. "Let our little guest get adjusted for a few minutes before you start bounding around." There were two bowls beside the door filled with food and water. I tried to get a drink, but Sally grabbed my ear. That was all I could take. I jumped at Sally and knocked her over. Soon the two of us were rolling on the kitchen floor, playing like we had been together all our lives.

Chapter 9

My Foster Home

The next few days went by quickly. My picture was taken for the ads to find a new home, and arrangements were made for a foster family to keep me until I would be adopted. My foster "Mommy" picked me up and drove me to her home, which was quite a long drive. I discovered this lady had two Shih Tzu dogs of her own and was a foster mommy to two others. All four dogs ran to meet me and started pouncing and playing with me.

It was a fun place to be. The other dogs were all black and white. I was the only champagne colored one. Foster mommy was really nice. The other dogs were all wearing t-shirts or sweaters that she had given them. She gave me a t-shirt too.

She also gave me a squeaky chicken toy. I really loved that chicken. It reminded me of the toys I used to play with at Nice Lady's house.

The next day, we went to the vet. I wasn't wearing my collar or any tags when I ran away so there was no way to know what shots I had. They were giving me all of them. The vet at the shelter had given me the first shots so the new vet just set dates to complete them. He also set a date to bring me in to be spayed. All rescue animals are spayed or neutered before they are adopted so they won't have puppies that will need homes.

Chapter 10

My Forever Mommy!

My picture and information were posted on the Internet. An application came in almost immediately from an elderly widow. Her references were checked, and someone visited her home. They felt this lady was the perfect forever mommy for me. I had my surgery to spay me and arrangements were made for my forever mommy to pick me up.

We were all playing in the fenced in back yard when the doorbell rang. Our foster mommy

called us in to meet my new forever mommy.
The other dogs ran to her, but I stayed behind. I
guess I was hoping it would be Nice Lady, but she
wasn't. I knew strangers weren't always nice,
and I wanted to be sure this lady would be good
to me.

She called me again, and I went over to her.
She patted me on the head. She seemed really
nice. I let her pick me up and she held me really
tight. She told me my new home was in the
country with lots of woods for us to take walks
in.

She signed some papers, and we were
ready to leave. Foster mommy said I could keep
my t-shirt and my squeaky chicken. She had

tears in her eyes when she hugged me and said

goodbye.

My new mommy put a leash on me and let me walk around before we got into her car. I sat on the seat beside her, and we drove off.

It was a really long ride to my new home. We stopped at a park along the highway when we were about half way home. I was on my leash, and we walked all around the park. I tried to chase a squirrel, but my new mommy said I shouldn't do that. I found out later, she already had a cat and I wasn't allowed to chase the cat either. I didn't like that at first, but when that old cat and I got acquainted, we snuggled together to take naps and rolled around and played every day.

I really love my forever mommy, and she loves me too. She talks to me all the time. We walk in the woods every day, and she buys me toys and treats, but she makes me mind too. She feeds the squirrels, but I'm not allowed to chase them. I'm just allowed to watch. I get pretty excited sometimes, and it's hard not to chase them, but I try not to.

I know I don't want to go away from my yard by myself. I like to go for walks on my leash.......and I love going for a ride in the car! Going out into the big world with my forever mommy is really exciting, but when I am alone, I love my fenced in yard.

I will never do that dumb thing again!

When I hear "sit", I will sit, and when I hear

"stay", I will stay!

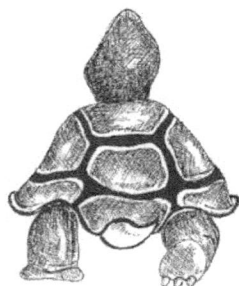

www.ingramcontent.com/pod-product-compliance
Lightning Source LLC
Chambersburg PA
CBHW051707090426

42736CB00013B/2582